Gardens, Gifts and Grace

Edited by Joyce Worsfold

First edition published in Great Britain in 2012

ISBN 978-1-909015-03-6
Published by Joyce Worsfold

2

Foreword

When creative Christians meet together anything can happen! Be it songs or sculptures, poems or paintings, banners, baking or carving wood. The Lord of creation inspires those who love Him, to be creators too. I'm not saying, for one moment, that those who do not believe, lack creativity. Just that those whose work is under-girded by prayer and worship probably create more often and for different purposes.

I have had the privilege, for many years now, to belong to two such groups; The Association of Christian Writers (A.C.W.) and the Quiet Garden Movement.

When A.C.W members meet together they worship, read the Bible, write together, inspire and encourage one another and most of all *pray* for each other. Prayer really *does* move mountains (or even writer's block!) They also laugh a great deal, share meals together and become part of each other's lives.

The Quiet Garden Movement is a simple ministry of hospitality and prayer launched in 1992 and now with over 300 affiliated homes and centres across five continents. It involves the occasional, sometimes permanent, provision of low cost, locally accessible places of welcome, reflection and gentle beauty. My home is one such Quiet Garden and over the years has been a place of warmth and refreshment for hundreds of people. For me, as a Quiet Garden host, it has been a great adventure that has given my husband and myself a lot of pleasure and has made for us many, very special, friends. Throughout the past 20 years I have visited many other Quiet Gardens and have, myself, been re-energised, cared for and blessed.

In this book these two strands come together and I hope that these readings might be as a 'quiet garden' for the reader; a place to dwell on the beauty of the natural world, a place of prayer, reflection and joy.

These pieces grew out of worship and are for worship, and like the five loaves and two fishes given by a small child to Jesus, they are our small, individual offerings that we pray He will use in His service.

Contents

God be your gardener

And make your soul a garden of

Refreshment when you are weary,

Deep peace when life is troubled,

Encouragement when you are disappointed

New growth, each season of your life.

Andrew Tawn

Thoughts for all Seasons.

In the ice blast of winter's death
enfold us deep in your dark and sleeping soil.
In the urgency of Spring's striving
quicken us to the awakening life within;
In the rich fullness and sweet breath of Summer
Unfold us as a flower, radiating Heaven's glory,
And in the autumn's journey towards rest
grant us gentle submission to your embrace, Lord God
the enduring presence through all our seasons.

Sarah Parkinson

Refreshing

Refreshing Lord of the Spring, drop rain into the lives of those who are in the depths of drought.
Shining Lord of the summer, bring warmth into the lives of those who are cold and lonely.
Colourful Lord of Autumn bring reds and golds into the lives of those who only see grey.
Sparkling Lord of the winter bring shining hope and shelter to those who are homeless.

Barbara Lightowler

Thank You

Great creator,
Oh, I want to thank you so much for Spring!
For balmy days when everything seems possible
For the heart-rending ballads of blackbirds
That slip sweetly through the air.
For carpets of crocus and spirited snow-drops.
For daffodils sparking a million smiles
and the polished petals of celandines.
For the blaze of tulips, vital and vivid
For burgeoning bluebells in tranquil woods
And exuberant blossom billowing trees.
O Lord I thank you for all of these.
For,the abundance of all your lavish gifts.
Help us Lord to slow down and savour
To lose ourselves in awe and wonder
For, all your astonishing grace.
Joyce Worsfold.

Irises at Giverney

Coaches belch out tourists
Spew onto asphalt
They wear hats, clutch cameras, hold handbags.
Channel, chattering through gates.
Then…extraordinary stillness
A collective sigh,
an ocean of iris,
a showy spectacle that staggers and stuns.

What pageant of perfection
What perfect paradigm
Vigorous violet with spills of wine
Crimson, claret, ruby and gold
Terracotta, umber and burgundy
Merge and meld, exquisite harmony.
Stop… stare and drink them in
Speckled, stippled, dappled and flecked
Each petal perfect, full-bloodied effect
Dazzle and drama
An impressionist painting
Heaven's own panorama
Unfolds and spools.

It's ours for creating…
We have the tools.

       Joyce Worsfold

"Then the Lord placed the man in the Garden of Eden to cultivate it and guard it" Genesis 2. !5

Snow-drops
February rains rinse them
White bells nod
Shiver in their splendour
In cold, earth clod.
Ice-gripped green-shoots
White,watch flowers
Star-stud emptiness
Touch holy hours.   J.W.

Winter Cobwebs.

Jack Frost and Spider
Perfect partners play
And create a silken filigree
Crunchy-iced embroidery
Enchant a winter's day.

J. W.

Tamed

Fierce. Rampant. Wild. Life.
Weeds clutch and claw the ancient tree
Rapier-sharp needles and poison darts
Guard caterpillars' black fruit.

But burned a greedy campaign
Stone on stone, chewed walls straightened
Fence posts bound in silver skirts
Piglets feast, uproot, devour.

Cleared, the field has grown
Backs ache, blisters bracelet palms
Thread thin shoots salute in crumbled soil
Tiny promises of harvest dreams.

K.B. Walker

Teamwork

It's dark, but you're still out there
Digging, building, pottering, doing,
'Doing too much!' I chunter from the settee
Wrestle with guilt coloured anger
Driven out to offer drinks, sandwich,
A telling off, 'Come in! Rest! Relax!'
He leaves his joy in mud-caked wellies
And comes in, for me.

K.B. Walker

Letting Go.

Wounded, I wander in the garden.
Fresh winds whip, the sting deserved.
Eyes scan but do not see
Till revealed by diamonds crossed.
Trellis supports, does not imprison.
Like the buddleia, I must launch you,
On, butterfly wings, into the world.

K.B. Walker

A Sonnet to Growth

Plant invasions, an unstoppable cause
Roots colonise, break through rock, cling, collide
Each plant breathes through microscopic pores
Each day absorbing carbon dioxide
Leaves pump out oxygen, energise souls
A cathedral of grasses and flowers
Triumphant sing, powerfully make whole
endless forests, fields and mountain power.

Plants warm others, releasing unseen gases
A chatter between them, all around air
Perfume and nectar assailing senses
Movement and colour a meadow prayer.
Each leafling a brother, each flower a bride
Transforming a bond, between all He provides.

J.Worsfold

The Greenhouse

I fling open the greenhouse windows and doors
Great gulps of Spring rush in, rush in

I scrub down the shelving, rub glass to a shine
crumble compost, pour seeds to hand's life-line

Scatter into the waiting womb.
Dead seeds from a darkened tomb
.
Roll vermiculite over it all
let the warming duvet fall.

Cover with a plastic pinnacle
And wait…. for… the miracle!

J.Worsfold

A Quiet Day

As I sat on the lawn on a windy Quiet Garden
Day several phrases came to mind.
Get rid of the cob-webs
Wrap up well
Face the wind
We shall not be moved
The final image is of a snow-shaker.
The idea is is that, sometimes in life
Things can come against us
And we can almost be blown off our feet,
But if we learn to put on the armour of God we will
Know the power of God, the Holy Spirit helping us
To be Shaken but not stirred.

Carole Pattenden

In the Garden at Westwood

The stillness, the peace, the wind
The rustling of the leaves in the trees
The many shades of green.
The horizon, the bare rugged hills in the background
The valleys with the villages nestling in them.
The buzz of bees in the bushes.
The majesty of the big trees, their trunks many years old.
The crunch of the gravel on the paths.
The perfumes and scents of the flowers.
The solidity and splendour of the church building
Standing proud above it all.
All these speak to me of God's love for His creation.

Jean Walmsley

In Times of Darkness

Bring me the rushing wind that roars
The ripped out roots and wild-swept moors
Seek where power is born.
Sing me the thunder of the seas
Sing me snowstorms, quietly
Where is the one whose love is torn?
Tremble the volcanoes fiery spews
Quiver me earthquakes terrible news
Show me the absolute core of peace
Weep me the withering waters wrench
Find me the flooded oozing stench.
Tell me, when will it cease?
Crumble before catastrophe,
Bend and bow to the one to be
And kneel before his face.
For we, informed and erudite
Are really useless in the fight
We live, but by His grace.
J.W

Commitment

Lord, sometimes I am not as close to you as I would like it to be
I stand aloof, afraid to commit,
afraid to give you my all in case I do not measure up, or you'll ask too much for me.
Help me to relax in your presence, to go with the flow and step in close
so that I can feel your breath.
Close enough for you to wipe the tears from my cheek
Close enough to feel your arms around me.
Close enough to feel safe.
Lord, please give me the strength and courage to draw on you   *Barbara Lightowler*

I Cannot Face the Future

I cannot face the future, Lord
It seems to much to bear.
How can I cope? Will there be hope?
Do you really care?

I do not want the months ahead –
Can I endure the pain?
All my fears stretch through the years
Will there be 'life' again?

'My child, I ask you just to *Trust*
and not the *see* the way.
Give me your hand, I'll help you stand
And give you hope each day.

To walk by faith and not by sight
Is what I want for you,
So lean on me and you will see
What I can really do.

I'll give you grace to meet your need,
but not before the day.
I'll give you hope so you *can* cope;
Believe I am the Way.

My promises are in my word
My child, I'll never leave you,
So courage take, I'll not forsake;
I am there, right beside you.
Kath Dredge.

For the Low in heart and mind

My friend, Christ knows just how you feel;
He's walked this way before.
He knows each feeling that you have;
He wants to help you more.
He wants to encompass you with love
And lift you out of pain
And put your feet upon the rock so you can stand again.
I know the feelings that you have;
His knowledge is far deeper –
He made us, formed us, loves us, spares us
He is God, our keeper.
So when you're weary, sinking low,
Call on the reigning King!
Begin to thank Him, praise His name –
He'll cause your heart to sing.
Kath Dredge

Thirsty

We are thirsty, Lord
Our souls are parched, cracked, dry.
The heat of hatred burns and blisters bodies
That seek to slake their thirst
But die.

We were thirsty, Lord.
Your death released
A deluge, a downpour, a flood.
Precious Lord, now you're here, on tap
Cool and clear, clear and cool
Refreshing, drenching, soaking
Giving back.

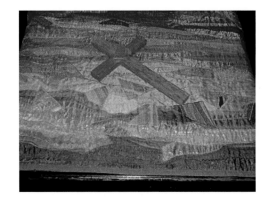

We are not thirsty, Lord
Supernatural sprinklers
Have quenched the flames
Water of life,
Name above all names.
You are our resevoir
Pure and deep.
Lord, soak us right through
Saturate, soak and steep.
Joyce Worsfold

Knowing God in the Everyday

Loving and restoring maker,
Help us to wait and search for You,
That we can be daring, hopeful and free,
As; Your healing spirit is timeless
Your flaming light is eternal,
Your Gentle Mercy is everlasting
And your endurance lasts for ever.
Alleluia! Come be with us O Jesus
In all our Everyday Lives.
Amen.

Written at Westwood Christian Centre
Linda Robinson

God's Gifts to you be

In your nature and of the moment

For helping others and for your own delight

To be used for the glory of God,

Special and unique to you.

Andrew Tawn

On Making Porridge

As I prepare the breakfast, Lord
Prepare me to meet You
In the mundane, the ordinary, the seemingly irrelevant.

As I soak the oats in water
Soak me with living water
Soften me, swell me with your love.

As I add milk and honey
Enrich me with Your sweet and gracious gifts.

As I stir the bowl
Please stir me up to serve You;
May the heating of the cereal
Reflect the warmth of your presence,
And as the mixture sometimes boils over,
Let your love overflow from me to all I meet.

As I cut up the banana,
May the fruits of the Spirit grow in my life,
And as I feel replete

'You open your hand and you satisfy all living things.
Thank you, Lord.

Jackie Hesketh

The Gift of Life…
Talitha Koum

I wish I had been a boy. They go to school and learn about everything. I think that my parents wish I'd been a boy as well. I can see that, because when they look at me sometimes, they have a sad, wistful expression. I've tried so hard to be obedient and quiet. Been seen and not heard.

Now is the time I'm seen and not heard for good.

I feel I've almost won something, but it's turned sour in my mouth. Now I know that they do love me. I can hear their hushed whispers, the catches in their throats, as they look at me in this quiet mausoleum room. Even my father, important as he is, sounds distraught and human. I feel that I could even call him 'Abba,' that is what my friends call their Daddy.

I cannot tell them how much I want to open my eyes and sit up and embrace them.
I feel like a butterfly trapped in a gilded cage for all the world to see. All those people who never noticed me before seem to parade their grief and show a morbid interest in every slight change of breathing, every slight fluttering of the eyelids. I don't feel shy now, only angry. Their pretended grieving is only intensifying the sorrow for my parents, wounding them deeper to the quick.

'Perhaps there is sin in your family that you haven't confessed, for why else would God punish you this way?'

The professionals are the worst. They wail and groan and make a mockery with their music. Only if I strain my ears can I hear in the background the faint notes of my friends, 'We played the flute for you and you did not dance.'

I feel frozen in death-like stillness. Early on I could feel my face prickle and sweat as the fever gripped. Now my living face has become a waxy immobile dial. My hair itches and scratches at my face as if begging to be noticed.

I am startled by the sound of children's voices in the distance playing and shrieking. Almost immediately they are signalled and silenced into a guilty hush out of respect for my plight.

I notice a change in the room. Something strange has happened. The room has lost the refreshing coolness of morning. There is a heady stickiness that you feel before a storm. Then I feel myself being swept away to a different place. I am one of many in a huge temple or palace. There is a large throne. A man sits there, smiling. A queue of people walk past the smiling man.

I hide behind a pillar and watch. I feel the coolness of the alabaster column against my cheek. The people are happy and seem to be glowing. Is it the reflection from their fine white garments? Or from the smiling man who is so dazzling in splendour. I'm desperate to join them, thrilled to be so close. An excitement verging on terror grips me. I am breathless. He smiles at me with His eyes and calls my name. I feel so heady, bursting with joy.

Then I'm on my bed again and someone is whispering gently in my ear,
>   'Talitha Koum, little girl, wake up!'
I open my eyes and try not to look at the face. I glance down at the calloused feet in dusty sandals. But I have to look up and know that I will see *that smile*.'

My stomach lurches and twists making a tremendous rumble. The man flings back his head and lets out a deep throaty laugh which is rich and velvety at the same time. He winks at me before turning his head to the small group of onlookers.

'Not dead, but only sleeping. Give her something to eat.'

He takes hold of my hand and the warmth of His life sweeps through me. He leads me to my parents. My father's face wears such a painful expression as if he dare not believe my wakening is true. The man says,

'Jairus here is your beloved daughter.'

Angela Coggins.

You can read this story in the Bible in *Luke, chapter 8 verses 40-56* and in *Mark, chapter 5 verses 21-43*.

Read slowly, perhaps repeating the reading several times. Savour each word. Certain words or phrases may jump out at you. If this happens you might like to meditate on them, asking God, 'What are you saying to me?' You might like to imagine yourself into the story. What do you see? You might like to be 'present' at other miracles. Why not try to 'imagine yourself into' any of the following readings.

- Jesus heals a boy with a demon. (Mark9. 14-29; Luke9.37-43a)
- Jesus calms the storm   (Matthew 8. 23-27, Mark 4. 35-41; Luke8.22-25)
- The man with a paralysed hand   (Matthew 12, 9-14; Mark 3.1-6; Luke 6. 6-11)
- Jesus feed five thousand men. (Matthew 14, 13-21, Mark 6, 30-44, Luke 9, 10-17, John 6, 1-14)

People

People are a pain – *that is my perception!*
After a busy day, I put my feet up!
The T.V. programme really is exciting
It's 9 o'clock, the phone rings – *people!*
People are peculiar – *that is my perception!*
They moan, they whine, they grumble all the time.
You organise a perfect outing for the church
And *still* they grumble – *people!*
People are a problem – *that is my perception!*
Albert did not like the woman preacher;
Peter thinks the leadership is wrong!
Yet no one will
take responsibility – *people!*
People are a pleasure – *that is my perception!*
I was struggling, feeling low, depressed;
I had preached my heart out - but for nothing.
Someone spoke encouragement – *ah people!*
People are a group to which I belong ,

There are many people and I'm one.
Am I a pain, peculiar, a problem?
Or do I bring pleasure when I come?

Richard Kay

Our Physical Gifts

Based on Mark 9. 38-end

What do you mean Lord?
If my hand causes me to sin
'chop it off!'
That's a bit melodramatic,
How can my hand cause me to sin?
Yes, I can see that I must be careful not to grab at things,
Not take all the food and money for myself,
Oh yes, and that expensive handbag on the shelf!
But what harm, upon my finger, a diamond ring
and gold
to have and to hold.
What? Diamonds and gold can become obsessions
What hurt we cause when we pile up possessions?
Mmm, I see what you mean.
My hands are a precious tool you've given
They can hug and hold and heal and feed,
stroke and carve and plant and weed.
But they can also be used to thump and scare
to hold a knife and scratch and tear.
Yes, I know what you are saying.

And my feet?
Yes, they can walk the extra mile
accompany a soul upon their journey
Take food and shelter to the hungry.
But..
They can also stamp and kick

Chase and march and terrify,
Yes Lord, I CAN see why.

And my eyes, Lord
I can choose what I see
I can see the hidden good in others
I can make them friends, sisters, brothers
I can see all the amazing abundance of this precious sphere
And I can see hunger, hatred and fear.

Oh Lord, draw my eyes away from what I desire and want
Use my hands to gently soothe and heal,
Use my feet to journey for you.
Help me to see and feel what is real
And all that I do, I'll try to do for YOU
For what you give is not counterfeit, but true.

Joyce Worsfold

You might like to contemplate all the physical gifts that you have been given, our five senses, the use of our hands and arms, legs and feet, our backs and shoulders, knees and elbows, etc.

- *Which are your strongest?*
- *Which do you use the most.?*
- *Which cause you problems?*
- *How might they lead you into sin?*

Some suggestions for Quiet Day Activities

> *Draw around your hand on a piece of paper. Inside the shape, make a list of all the things that you use your hands for*

On the outside of the shape, write down the things you would like to use them for but haven't done recently.

Why is this?

You might like to do the same with your feet.

Are there things you have done with them that you regret? You might like to confess these and ask God for forgiveness.

You might like to write a prayer, poem or letter to God, thanking Him for your hands or feet or senses etc.

If there is a part of your body that is particular painful or that needs healing in some other way,
Prayers for healing might be shared.

The Gift of Sight

It's dark
It's always dark
Deep dark
No spark
Sitting in smothering dust
Powdered on lips caked on tongue grit in eyes,
the infernal stench
Of bodies always rushing on urgent errands.
In my deep dark I am invisible to all.

Inside me there is a light

that leaps
that sings.
But they are blind
and I imprisoned
by helpless eyes.

Blazing heat
sears flesh
dries lips
no drink.

Flat patter of sandals,
childrens's feet
gabble, prattle, jabber
clamber up the hill.
A moving tide of excitement
He's coming, coming, coming…
The vibrato breaks
Here, here, here
The light inside cracks open
My voice hurled through the steaming air,
'Jesus, Son of David, have pity on me!'
'Shut up beggar!' they pounce.

'Son of David!' I scream
my once only chance
'Have PITY!!!'
The stillness of awe,
A monumental hush
A gentle swish of movement
'Bring him to me'

Strong hands lift and lead
Warm fingers cup my cheeks
'What do you want me to do for you?'
I feel his electricity
Trace sparks in my soul,
'Sir, I want to see again
I speak my heart's deepest yearning
His fingers velvet my eyes
'Then see, your faith has made you well'

I see
His eyes
And know
All love
And I praise and praise, praise and praise!

Joyce Worsfold

Sorry

I've messed up and broken faith
Lost the way fallen from grace
I did it wrong and meant it too
I've broken my word and left the truth
I didn't think, didn't care
Walked quite blind into the snare
So now I'm trapped and alone and scared.

I'm sorry, so sorry
Please restore, please forgive
Please grant again that I may 'live'
Put your hand again on me
Release your peace, release your love
Bring down your blessing from above
I can't promise to be good
And keep myself from all falsehood.

I have sinned, I have failed
The one I love I have betrayed.
I repent and I turn back
God make up the right I lack
Break my heart, break my pride
I'm so ashamed that I lied
That I forgot that Jesus died
To set us free and make us right
Give us life, power and might
To love and serve aright.

Susan North

Gifts of Forgiveness and Compassion

The Little Maid   (2 Kings 5. 1-15)

Here I am, in a country not my own, captured, abused, far away from all I love and forced to wait upon a soldiers wife.

I should hate them, despise them, be filled with terrible anger and yet, here I am full of…deep concern.

　'Why God? Why?'

Why should I care that he is covered with weeping sores, his flesh eaten daily, rotting and stinking? Surely it's what he deserves.

I avert my eyes when she tenderly bathes his wounds as I stand and hold the bowl. But the love between them rushes at me, surrounds me, soaks into my soul.

'Why should I care?'

But I do. Oh! My Lord and my God has filled me with…pity? Concern? Empathy? *Love?*

Oh God, what do you want of me?
to love my enemy?
To actually love the people who dragged me to this place?
It is too much to ask and yet…
I feel a boldness sweeping through me,
words that have to be spoken tumble into my mouth.

'If only my master would see the prophet who is in Samaria. He would cure him of his leprosy!'

There, I've said it. I sounded so sure, how could that be?
I called him, *'my master'* this man I have so much reason to hate.
From where did come such humility?
I watch the dejected, disfigured man raise his head, straighten his back, stand tall.
I watch the dull eyes, lighten.

I see the hope that I have seeded take root and begin to grow
And I know that my God is right here, with me still.
In this far off miserable place, *I am home.*
Joyce Worsfold

The Gift of Family

Who are my mother and brothers?   (*Matt. 12, 46-50, Mark3, 31-33, Luke 8. 19-21*)
The growing crowd gathered and peered,
pursuers and petitioners
streamed around Him like a lake
lost fragments of loveliness.

Gaunt faces stretched with pain
wrinkled like ribbons wreathing flesh.
Some with weary malnourished walk
Pale as wax with unlit wicks.

And in the midst of all… My Son!
Speaking sunlight, healing hurt
Here *We* are!
Some have said things that cracked and chipped my sense of self

Some pressed thorns to pierce my heart
and hurled their words like ropes to fasten
Snuffing -Out -Certainties-
I needed to see Him,
I just wanted a word
'Mum' would have done,
But I should have known.
'Who is my Mother?'
The words drenched the loaded air
Leering faces sneered and sniggered
'Who are my brothers?'
BUT…
His arms reached out to circle all
'Here is my mother and my brothers!'
His face leaked love
His arms were power and light
It was as if He held *us* tight,
Our hearts healed
Our longings filled.
My soul's sweetest song
His eyes clung to mine
And rich air dazzled.
I could smell the sweet breath of His goodbye
And was pierced by inexplicable joy!

Joyce Worsfold

Naomi

They are dead. All dead. And so am I, though I still breathe.
This grief-razed place is mine no more.

"Go home. Go back," I urge. "Leave. Start again," I beg.
But she will not.

Her sister, yes, and I am glad. Glad as empty chaff can be.
But she will not.

Where you go, I go, your home, mine. Your God is my God,
Was all her broken heart would say.

In silken whispers the desert feeds on endless tears.
Yet sand still burns blistered toes.

In cloth of sack and ash-smeared face, declare disgrace and curl up to die.
But she will not.

In sun and shame she bends and gleans. The least, the last,
She is seen and brings me grain.

Her light pierces selfish dark, till, turned from festered wounds,
I see her new.

Bathe, perfume, instruct. A rish, a hope, a gift laid at his feet.
Breath held, the sandal speaks.

She will know joy.
And so will I.

Kimm Brook

For the Gift of New Beginnings

Zaccheus (Luke 19, 1-9)
This meditation can be used as part of an Easter reflection.(just add the last 3 lines)
In our imaginations let's sit at the foot of the cross and imagine all the people Jesus has helped
standing there, looking up at his torn and wounded body. How would they have felt, grief-filled?
Unbelieving? Lost? Screaming out, 'Why?

O God, I don't understand this!
Here I am on a hillside
Watching Him die,
Why?
It's such a little time since He came to Jericho
Hours, days, just a short time ago.
O God!
I am a little man
Small in stature with a wizened mind
I've loved and cherished *me*
Beyond all reason
Leaving everyone else behind.
My things, *my* status, *my* work
How I've plotted and schemed
Calculated and conspired
Of myself only have I dreamed
There's been such a canker in my soul
He made me feel valued
In just a moment He made me whole.

I stamped on and bullied those I met
Used them as a ladder to reach right to the top
Chief tax collector, that's me and yet

Now I've reached those dizzy heights
Executive director, master of all
I find myself perverted, polluted and realise
I've heard no-one's desperate call.

Oh I knew all the ruses, dodges and tricks
to build my private empire of gold and bricks.
Fine wines, smart suits, designer goods,
Fountains, flowers, silks and cedarwoods
And still there was more.
More to yearn for.
A yawning hole to be filled
A desperate longing to be stilled.
Taut nerves, disturbed mind, angry heart.
Self-made loneliness crushing me
No-one liked what had grown to be.
I became a man apart
No-one's friend, no one's lover
No one's special one
No one's brother.
No mishaps, no real pain or grief
Just…emptiness for this cunning thief.

When I first heard his name I was all stirred up
Something shifted right deep inside
And I left the office, didn't even lock up
I lifted my robe and ran
Suddenly possessed, about seeing this man.
I ran to get ahead of the crowd
A buzzing beat about my ears.
The clamouring throng was loud,

I stood on tip-toe in a vain attempt to see
And was crushed and pushed towards an overhanging tree.
I leapt and climbed with a strength I'd never known before
And lay along the arching bough.
Suddenly I glimpsed the man
And my world pivoted, skipped and spun
There was a silence about my ears
And from deep within a well of tears
And looking down through the blur of years
I saw myself,reflected in his eyes
And glimpsed all that I could learn to prize.
Beauty, joy, love and light
Creation made for my delight
He stopped,
He looked
Full into my face
And said
Zaccheus, I'm coming round to your place
And all I had seemed meaningless and poor
The moment that he, walked through my door

But now this……this cross, this hill, this darkling place, this great grief
This tearing place.
WHY?

Joyce Worsfold

The Gift of Inclusiveness

Crumbs of Comfort (Matthew 15 v21-28)

Here we go again. Hotfooting it out of trouble. Following Jesus has led us into some tight spots recently. For example by facing up to the Pharisees Jesus has ruffled their feathers again. Why can't they just accept him and call Him Lord instead of nitpicking around the rule books. Jesus has given it to them straight how empty their faith is, all words and rules and blooming ablutions. I thought we were going to head off to somewhere a bit quieter where we can give ourselves some space. Jesus loves to sit and wait and sit some more and share some thoughts about life and the Father. However that's not to be. This takes the biscuit though. Instead of the backwaters of Galilee we've walked up to heathen territory. Canaan, of all places. Perhaps Jesus thinks we'd be less of a crowd drawer up there. Anyway I guess he needs to recover after doing that amazing miracle feeding all those hungry folk, 5,000 and all!

And then, just when we've got ourselves sorted, somewhere quiet like, she comes running down the hillside wailing like she's lost something precious, a Canaanite woman, I ask you. I know Jesus likes to listen to everyone, waifs and strays and whatever, but this is too much! A Canaanite woman! Who does she think she is barging in and talking to Jesus, she's from a long line of Baal worshippers for goodness sake. And you know how disgusting their practices are, child sacrifice for one thing. She's on her own, another bad sign, and she won't take no for an answer. Mind you, she seems to know who she's shouting at – 'Son of David.' That's unusual, I've not heard any call him that, 'cept Peter. Distraught and driven to distraction she is, as if this is the final shot at saving her demon destroyed daughter. She looks like she's working herself up to put everything into this encounter with Jesus, with the Lor'Son of David!' How does she know? How come the Pharisees don't address Jesus like that? It would be so much smoother. No ruffled feathers or phylacteries! Anyway our lovely Lord just stares at her, at then looks right at us; waiting, anticipating our response perhaps. Well we've been here before - dealing with the undesirables. Mind you that's a word I've never heard Jesus utter! A few of us, nearest the woman, just look at her as if she's something they've just stepped in. I can see it written all over their faces – another public relations disaster. Some of my mates look shifty and a bit disconcerted and embarrassed. You can tell they're thinking she's not one of us and we should keep ourselves separate from contamination, a Canaanite woman! Thinking it over it reminds me a bit of how the Pharisees are – looking at the outward stuff. Complaining about contamination.

 This is getting interesting. If I know Jesus even a little bit he's going to turn everything on its head. Hang on a minute things aren't going according to plan. Some of us disciples have begged Jesus to get rid of her and send her on her way. She isn't part of the big story. She's just staring at Him and he's looking at her in a sort of complicit way as if he and she are sharing something the rest of us don't follow. Then Jesus looks over and speaks to us in a sort of questioning way.

"I was sent only to the lost sheep of Israel ."

He's seems to be provoking us to limit His mission. He then just smiles at her and sort of nods as if he wants her to join in and continue. She sinks to her knees and sums up everything that anyone's ever asked Jesus, so succinct!

"Lord, help me".

Well it's a powerful moment and I can feel something special and deep about to break through.
Though when he utters the words it's like a massive surprise –he's almost speaking aloud what we're thinking- we've enough to do sorting out our own lot. But Jesus says,

"It is not right to take the children's bread and give it to the lap dogs".

 Mind you he's been a bit gentle describing the Canaanites like that, almost affectionately, I've heard them being described a lot worse, Pet puppies indeed! It's enough to send some of the hard liners into a mouth froth. And yet, and yet- I don't think he even means it – he's like underlining his main mission but not his only mission. Comfort and hope for all folk not just children of Abraham and followers of Moses. By now the woman's just looking into His face and gazing at Him smiling- as if she's in on the lesson for all the bystanders.

"Yes Lord, but even pets eat the crumbs that fall from their masters' table."

Jesus beams and that is some sight to see. We just melt and marvel. What just happened? Does that mean all bets are off and Jesus' message goes beyond what we thought – that the Pharisees can take it or leave it and we should concentrate on those who can recognise Jesus, even the Canaanites?

"Woman you have great faith! Your request has been granted."

Well all this talk about food is making me a bit peckish, what's next on the agenda? Oh right, Jesus says we,ve got another 4,000 to cater for, bread for everyone!

Angela Coggins

The Gift of Prayer

'Come with me by yourselves to a quiet place and get some rest'

Matthew 5. v 44	'But now I tell you: love your enemies and **pray** for those who persecute you'
Matthew 6. 5-15	'When you **pray** do not be like the hypocrites' (also Luke 11.2-4)
Luke 11, 1-13	Jesus' teaching on prayer. (also Matt. 6. 9-13 and 7. 7-11)
Matthew 18 .1-8	'always **pray** and never become discouraged'
Matthew 14. 19b	He looked up to heaven and gave thanks to God (feeding of Five thousand.
Matthew 14 23	'After sending the people away, he went up a hill by himself to (mark 6.46,) pray.
Luke 9.18	'One day when Jesus was praying alone his disciples came to Him'
Luke 22.32	'But I have prayed for you, Simon, that your faith will not fail'
Luke 22. 41-45	'Then he went off from them about the distance of a stone's throw and knelt down' And 'Get up and pray that you will not fall into temptation.' (Also Matt. 26. 36-46: Mark 14.32-42.)
John 17. 1-26	Jesus prays for his disciples

For Christians, one of the most precious gifts is being able to spend time listening to God and talking to him. In the Bible we find Jesus, over and over again, going off by himself, or with friends and spending time with God. If Jesus needed to do this, how much more is it a need for us. It can be tempting to think that there are 'good' and 'bad' people, confident that we are in the good category because we haven't done anything too terrible. And what about Judas? He wanted his way, not God's way. Is that so unusual? If we dismiss him as pure evil, will we learn from his mistakes?

Judas

'For in his own eyes he flatters himself too much to discover and hate his sin'

Chosen, one of the chosen brothers,
Dropped his life and followed,
Like the others.

Witnessed miracles beyond record
Suffering eased, sins forgiven
Hope offered, faith restored.

Sent to the harvest fields,
Along with the rest,
He ministered, taught, healed.

Why couldn't Jesus see,
It wasn't enough? With *power*
The Messiah was meant to free.

Betrayed to provoke, lest
He failed to understand,
Judas knew best.
What's that to do with me?

Kimm Brook

A Busy Day

It has been a gruelling morning
Jesus in Capernaum
Preaching in the synagogue.
People, amazed, enthralled.
Such a stillness there is,
You could hear a pin drop.
He isn't your usual teacher of the law
He really knows the scriptures
Backwards, forwards, upside down
They are part of him
And he speaks with such love, passion and authority.
People lean forward to hear Him better
And God stirs in them
The spirit moves over them.

Suddenly the door crashes open
A mad man comes running
There are gasps of horror, fear festers
He screams ferociously
 'What do you want with us, Jesus of Nazareth?'
He carries on alarming, threshing and screeching
Oozing aggression from every pore.

Jesus is so calm
He orders the evil spirit
 'Be quiet! Come out of the man!'
It does.
The place buzzes, everyone agog, fired up, disturbed.
 'Come round to my place' says Simon

So Jesus and his friends go straight there
Looking forward to a bit of peace and a Sabbath lunch.

The house has a strange hush.
It's inhabitants talk in whispers
And worry
Simon's Mum in law is sick
She's got a raging temperature
She's in a right state.

Jesus goes straight to her
And takes her hand.
It's like a cool stream flowing
The headache, the burning, the tossing and turning
are no more
He helps her up
And immediately she bustles about
Getting lunch.

They relax
The sun sets
It's been a long day.

Then…
Simon stares out of the window and gasps
A sea of people in every direction
The blind, the deaf, disabled and disturbed
Imploring Jesus to help.

And of course… he does
A child with club-feet, a baby with a withered arm

A woman with disfigured face,
A man with constant pain
Still he ministers,
Tenderly touching
holding, hugging, cleansing calming
Until darkness falls
And slowly, they return to their homes.
They sleep…and Jesus? He prays.

So much to be done
But when He discusses with His Dad
In the early hours, in a peaceful place
He knows what He has to do.

Jesus! Jesus! ? We want Jesus
Simon seeks Him urgently,
'Lord! Where have you been? They're all waiting'

I have to go, I have to tell everyone
About my Father
There is so little time…

J.Worsfold

Fast Living.

We are choosing the faster tiring lane
Not the slow crawler lane
For the lame, broken, boring
The awkward misfits who,
don't really belong.
Our time is too precious – can't you see?
We're so talented: we can do so much
You'd better not hinder our plans.
We might feel vulnerable, if you stood in the way,
Make us angry, impatient and sharp,
Tell you the rules we would,
Forget you've heard them all before,
Forget the God wastes His time on us
Until, when broken, we hear his call.
Susan North

The Gift of Jesus

Meditation of the Angel   (Luke 1, 26-38

Hello, I'm Gabriel an angel of the Lord. One day God called to me and said that I should go to Mary of Nazareth to give her some very, very important news. I was really excited because although we visit people on earth all the time they don't always see us. But this time God wanted me to speak with Mary face to face.

He knew of course that she would be frightened, human beings are always a bit scared when they see one of us. So he gave me very careful instructions. The first words I had to say were, "don't be afraid"

Mind you when God told me what was going to happen I was afraid myself. " I am going to send my son" he said "to earth as a human being" He shook his head sadly and there was such pain in His eyes, it really frightened me.

Then He told me the rest of the plan and I was terrified, I mean we all were! You see we love Jesus, he's amazing and wonderful, absolutely the best. And God was going to send Him to you on earth and we all know what human beings are like! Don't we. I mean they can be lovely but God gave them all free choice. Imagine that, human beings can choose to do whatever they want and that causes SO many problems. They argue and fight and even kill one another. They're greedy and bad tempered and they gossip and they can be very cruel. And God was planning to send Jesus to them!

Whats more, he wasn't going to send Jesus as a grown up who could look after Himself! Jesus was going to be born in the same way that human babies are. Risky!! Not only that, He was going to be born in a war zone. Is God mad!

"You can't do that" I said " They'll hurt Him, they might hit him and shout at Him, they might even kill Him"

" I know" said God shaking His head wearily "But its the only way to save them"

" But you love Him" says I.

"I love them too" said God "Every single one of them, I love them with all my heart" His voice broke then and tears poured down His cheeks. " Now go" He said. "Go and tell Mary the Good News!"

Where is the Christmas Child ?

'Oh where is the baby?'
The old folk cry
Beneath years of nostalgia,
Sentiment piled high.
Oh where is the baby we used to know
When Christmas was simple
without all this show?
Where is the baby?
That once lived here
Where is the baby?
He is lost I fear.

'Oh where is the baby?
The middle-aged cry
Beneath all the baubles
And presents piled high
Where is the baby?
Beneath mountains of cards
And glitter and booze
Christmas is hard.
Where is the baby?
Not in my back yard!

Where is the baby?
Of this winter feast
Did anyone see
His star in the east?

Don't offend anyone
With Nativity scenes
With Peace and hope
and love and dreams.
We all live together
But, side by side
Oh where is the baby?
I can't decide.

Here is the baby
Not patiently lying
But outside and suffering,
Outside and dying
It's him you hear knocking
Hard at the door
It's Him in Somalia
cold on the floor.
Where is the baby?
He grew and He died
He suffered for you and he suffered for me
Where is the baby, just let me see
For I know
His love is amazing, fantastic… and free.
Come and see.
J.W.

Nativity

For unto us a Child is born

In the dark, weary spirits rush, laden beneath busy-ness
Consider the reason

Unto us a Son is given

Worries seep through obligation's rough wool. Has enough been done?
Listen to the meaning.

And His name shall be called Wonderful

In the emptiness, cracks glow between worldly bricks piled high.
Feel the melody.

And, lo, the Angel of the Lord came

Sing the barriers down. God's glory blazes from hope-filled faces.
Join in. All are welcome

Good tidings of great joy

Face the light without fear. Made new in the promise, the gift, love.
Glory to God in the highest, and on earth peace, good will toward men.

Kimm Brook

The Gift of Salvation

'There were many women there, looking on from a distance, who had followed Jesus from Galilee and helped Him. Among them were Mary Magdalene, Mary the mother of James and Joseph, and the wife of Zebedee.' (Matthew 27. 55,)

Mary Magdalene

O my Lord, How did it come to this?
My dear friend
These feet on which I perfume poured
And tenderly dried with my hair
Now, bloody, wounded and deformed,
So sore and swollen
Hanging there.
These feet which once
Walked on water
And endless roads
Seeking and searching
For forgotten souls,
Pinioned and pierced.
Nails through sinews
Nails through bone.
These feet that I once kissed
Now I cannot even hold.

O Lord, those eyes
That hold all anguish, burning pain
Would that they would look at me again.
Me, soiled and spat at
Defiled and desecrated
Used, abused and bruised.
Yet you saw what God created

You looked at me with
Respect
And all my devils
Left.

O Lord, your hands
Pierced, impaled, grotesque
Hands whose thumbs
Massaged spittle to unseeing eyes
And made the blind to see
Your hands
Broke bread
Blessed babes
Brought peace
Caused the raging storm
to cease.

Parched cracked lips
cry, 'I thirst'
I long to
Hold cold
water for your sips.
My heart bursts.
They dip a sponge in bitter gall
And thrust it near your face
And jeer as you try to drink
In this horrific darkened place.

They want to
extinguish the Light

To quash, to quell
To destroy, to douse
All the good and right.
Devour the bread
Wash the water away
Vanquish the vine
Exterminate today!
 "Forgive them for they know not what they do"
Even now!
Master, even now!
You… Forgive!
 "It is finished!"
The Life it leaves
Is this ALL there is?
                                        J.Worsfold

Mary at the Cross

'Standing close to Jesus' cross were his mother, his mother's sister, Mary the wife of Clopas and Mary Magdalene. Jesus saw his mother and the disciple who Jesus kloved standing there; so he said to his mother, 'He is your son.'
Then he said to the disciple, she is your mother.' From that time the disciple took her to live in his home.'
 (John 19.27)

My Lord, My God
What is happening here
This hill, this cross, this hopelessness
I am paralysed and powerless
Yet still I watch.
This is my son, my beloved one
The fruit of my womb which you created.
On those hands, which I so often held in mine
Crushed, distorted, broken
On those feet that pattered after me so trustingly
Nailed through flesh, through muscle and bone.

Father you are my rock, my protector, my strong tower
Hold me now
This is so hard to bear.

Was it for this the angel came?
I didn't know how he would come to be
But you, who gave birth to ice and flame
Who knits together bones without surgery
Who makes deaf men hear and the blind to see,
Your spirit over-shadowed me.

Giving birth was such joy
Depite the pain
Holding him to my breast
His downy head, sweet breath.
Seeing him play
Watching him grow.
My home, his home
His joy my joy

His sadness, mine
His life, my life.

Listen everyone
That's my son
In all of this he thinks of me
He came to heal the broken hearted
He came to set YOU free
He came to lead you out of the wilderness
Away from your own rootlessness.
To show you love, to give you peace
Why did you not listen?
He is looking at me
And such love radiates through his agony
In all of this, He thinks of me'
 'John, here is your mother,
mother, here your son'

My soul declares the greatness of the Lord
He is the Son of God
My saviour, my redeemer
Your saviour, your redeemer
He has accomplished what he set out to do.

I am the Lord's servant
May it be to me as you have said.

Joyce Worsfold

Atonement

Golden flowers line the road
Gold is for a King
The road the only way
To remember Easter day
The incense of sacrifice
Rises like a prayer
The smell of suffering
Is heavy in the air

The faithful gather round
At eventide they pray
Bewildered and afraid
As God is betrayed
Shrouds of night close in
Darkness fills the air
Walk this way softly
In silence and prayer

Come, come with your load
The pain and strife
For the road is penitence
And death the way to life
The guilty are condemned
And death the punishment
It's my death, but His life
For he, not I, paid the price.

Susan North

God so loved… that He gave…
John 3.16, Rom.12.1

The ultimate love gift

His own precious Son;
What more could he give
than the All-Perfect one?

Can I show God's love?
To love is to give
In time and in talents
The way that I live,
But still something more
It's to nail to the cross
My desires and ambitions
And count them all loss
And present myself daily
To Him (who first gave)
As a sacrifice, living,
An obedient slave.
And to count it all joy
To give, not to gain,
Longing only to serve Him
The lamb who was slain.

God so loved…that he gave
His own precious Son.
How can *my* love compare
With what He has done?

Kath Dredge

57

Thankfulness

For all love and kindliness
All that's true, right or best
In life that overflows
In darkness a hope still glows
Shines and leads aright
ever onwards to daylight.
For all friends and times spent
And moments out of heaven sent
For all of these and everything in thanks,
O Lord, ourselves we bring.
Susan North

The Gift of a Sound Mind

"When they saw Jesus they pleaded with him to leave their region"

How many pigs charged into the lake and drowned? The whole bloody lot – that's how many. Fifty we reckoned, though my cousin says it was more like two thousand! Yes, the two mad guys are better apparently, but I'll believe that when they have done an honest days work – and stick at it for a year or two. I don't believe in this demon possession nonsense; they were just a couple of crazy guys who could scare the shit out of you if you upset them. People here knew to leave them alone, give them some food and keep off their patch – not too difficult when they lived in a graveyard! Then this other lunatic, who knows nothing about our village or our ways of doing things, charges in with a load of hangers-on and damn near gets killed when Biff and Bash (God knows what their names are; everyone calls them Biff and Bash) start their ranting and raving. I don't know exactly what happened next, but the long and the short of it is the pigs get the wind up, charge down the hill and drown in the bloody lake. Biff and Bash were pretty impressed by all accounts, clapped and cheered and said they felt better than they had ever felt. The poor sods looking after the pigs came and told me what had happened and what was I going to do about it? Soon everyone knows, and they want me to go and see this idiot and make sure he doesn't hang around our village. God knows what he would be up to next. So off I went with practically the entire bloody village behind me.

"Excuse me. Sir," I said. "Do you mind moving on? This is private property."

He turned out to be one of these religious fanatics. Quietly spoken, I must admit, but all he wanted to talk about was God and hoping we would help these two mad guys now that they were better. I asked him point blank: "Did you frighten those pigs so that they stampeded into the lake?"

"Not exactly," he said. "It is more complicated than that. Think about your demons," he said.

Bloody cheek, I thought. "What demons?" I said.

"We have all got demons," he said. "Demons of selfishness, demons of greed, demons of fear, demons tempting us to do what we know is wrong."

Here we go, I thought. He's a bloody nutter.

"Well," he said, "when these two brothers of mine….."

Brothers! He had never clapped eyes on them before.

"…. When I saw their distress," he said, "I needed to show them that God doesn't just want them restored, God wants them to know that when He deals with a problem, the problem is dealt with once and for all. It is the same with sin," he says.
I knew he'd get on to that! They are all the same, these preachers. Sin, sin. That's all they bloody talk about.

"Well," he said, "if you repent, God will not just accept your repentance, He will remove your guilt; drown it in the sea; give you a fresh start."

I nearly said, "Lake, you mean. There are no seas round here, mate" but I let it pass. Anyway, to cut a long story short, he asked me if they could stay a while and talk some more about the kingdom of God. He'd have probably stayed a bloody fortnight if we'd let him.

"No," I said. "We'd be grateful if you would get on your way."

He just sat there.

"Please," I said. "I'm the village leader, and we just want to be left alone. Now, please be on your way."
He got up from the bank he was sitting on.

"It has been an interesting day," he said, "and a pleasure to meet you all."
Actually, we should at least have offered him and his friends some food before they set off, but they didn't ask for any, so we didn't give them any. We were keen to see the back of them.

I arranged a whip-round to pay for the bloody pigs.
He was a funny bloke.
Who does he think he is, any way? I wonder

Robin Carmichael

God grant you his generous gifts of grace,

Riches beyond price, yet freely given;

Abundant life, unconditional love

Countless blessings, perfect peace,

Enduring hope and joy without end.

Andrew Tawn

God's Riches At Christ's Expense

'For it is by God's grace that you have been saved through faith. It is not the result of your own efforts, but God's gift so no-one can boast about it.'
Ephesians 1

'My grace is all you need, for my power is greatest when you are weak'
(2 Corinthians 12.9a)

<u>'There but for the grace of God go I'</u>

Being Adrose Together

I try to hide my crinkled nose in a smile of greeting. The carer turns to lock the door behind me, a solid barrier against the fresh spring breeze outside. Over-warm air, heavy with smoke, industrial strength cleaning products and the indignity of adults in nappies, encases me.

Through another locked door I greet a wraith, mumbling and loitering near this escape route. He brings his face within an inch of mine. Puffing and blowing, his breath is sour and his manner threatening to the uninformed. I shake his hand and say his name. The skin feels cool even in this warm place and stretched smooth across bony fingers. He smiles and turns away.

Peeping into a small lounge, the curtains clean but pulled awry, my eyes rest on a wheelchair bound soul with sightless eyes in a saggy, basset hound face. His hands are cupped together on his lap. 'Sweetie please?' he says.

'Sorry, Fred, I don't have any sweeties today.'

The other occupant, a long lean man dressed in a rugby shirt, his distorted frame supported by brightly coloured cushions and a child's cow shaped furry backpack. In his silent world, chin locked onto his chest, even smiles are denied. His wife, so often by his side, is not there today and concern for her recurring bouts of depression flares across my mind.

I am drawn then to the far end of the long corridor, past the staff room. Recollections of a hundred tiny kindnesses, a gentle kiss, a cuddle, a dignity respected, lift my spirits.

Determined, Rose plods past me on her never-ending circuit of the passageway. Her hand grips the safety rail that runs its length. I shout a greeting and smile.

'Eh? What'd you say?' she bellows in return.

'Hello Rose,' I raise my voice another decibel and smile as widely as I can.

In the large L-shaped lounge I notice the new carpet and an elderly man trying to pick the pattern off. The ragged armchairs have been replaced with stylish, matching ones and I feel grateful that these things are deemed important but not at the expense of the care given.

Wartime music is pulsing loudly and Hattie swishes up to me with an infectious but toothless grin. I bend, as she presses her soft, road-map-lined forehead to mine and says, 'Do you want to dance, Sally?'

Holding her hand, I sway and smile. She lifts her skirt above her knees and dances a little dance for me, all the time telling tall tales about Charlie and Sally and whispering about the mischief we used to get up to. Then she moves away to another Sally or Charlie, lighting dark corners with her bright memories.

At last I spot the one I seek. She's in a corner asking incomprehensible questions to one unable to answer. Her fingers work incessantly, brow furrowed deeply and scarred where she's fallen in her anxiety, rushing nowhere on frail legs.

'Hello Mum.' I touch her arm and bend to place my face in her narrow line of vision.

'Ahhh,' she smiles, as she sees that I am one of hers.

'Shall we go up to your room?' I ask, leading her towards the locked door. A carer struggles with a cluster of keys to let us out.

'How's life clipping you?' Mum asks.

'I'm fine, Mum,' making sure I smile because the words have no meaning now.

'One of the, I was going to say, what are?' she asks, her body language indicating she wants an answer.

'This lift is noisy,' I reply. Her muscles are tense and fingers still chattering.

'Thought you were making yourself dilling.'

'Come into the lift, Mum.' There is no recognition of her image in the large mirror that dominates the tiny space.

She cannot understand my directions and resists physical prompts so it takes ages to negotiate our way to her room. It is clean and tidy, photographs of her children and grandchildren dotted around. Her mattress is on the floor so that when she falls out in the night she won't hurt herself. Bars would only frighten her. A soft throw over the two-seat settee, a pretty cushion and teddy bears are tactile attempts to comfort and reach into her muddled mind.

'I've looked at that miline one,' she tells me.

'Shall we sit here for a while, Mum?' I sit down and try to manoeuvre her beside me.

'We'll have to be adrose together.' For a moment she is quiet and looks at the floor, as if lost.

'It's a lovely day, Mum.'

'Oh hello, luv. I keep forgetting.' She smiles, seeing me, as if for the first time. 'How are for?'

I tell her in snatches about her son and other family news using pictures to help her remember but it has gone. She can only listen in tiny bursts but chatters happily, her muscles slowly relaxing, her hands finally still.

The photos and her hands remind me of the long hours of work she did in the mills and at home rearing six children. The muscular calves made large from walking miles in the Yorkshire hills and valleys have disappeared from her skeletal frame. The gaunt face barely resembles her smiling one captured in the photographs. Her heart was more than equal to making room for me, the other wives and husbands and the many grandchildren. I remember her saying that it was important for parents to have a regular time together, backed up by the offer of free babysitting. I can hear her laughter and smell the roast chicken, mashed potatoes and gravy, puddings swimming in custard that we often shared on those Friday nights before we went out.

Her common sense advice, only ever offered on request, support and encouragement filled the void of my own mother's loss.

'Can I have some artimicial?' she asks. I search in her drawer and find some chocolate. 'Mmmm,' she murmurs as I put a piece into her mouth. She gives me a chocolaty, coquettish grin.

'Is that nice?' I giggle with her.

'They seem very enjoyed by each other,' she adds. As she tires, I take her back downstairs where she will be whisked into her pyjamas by skilled hands.

Mum smiles into the familiar face of the friendly carer and forgets that I've been.

I know better than to say goodbye, as the ache of parting would remain even if she couldn't remember why. I wait beside the locked door to be set free, sign myself out and hurry back into the springtime.

K.B.Walker,   An excerpt from my memoir, **A Life Less Lost'**

Lost Chord

Shadows in the darkness
People stretched around
Cocaphoney of voices
Dissonant sound.
Violet waits.

Soft wool of cardigan
Rough cord of skirt
Smoothness of buttons
Slotting into holes
Violet rubs
Over and over, soft and smooth
Violet's mind in a touching groove.

Sun streaming through window
People sitting round
Shouting and calling
Discordant sound
'I want my tea'
'Get away from me'
They sit
They wait
For something.

The door it opens
Wind blows in
Youth glows on faces
And moves in them.
Unzip a polished cello
Tuck viola under chin
Residents excitement
Is creeping in
'We're going to have some music!'
'We can sing !'

Cradling his cello

He kneels by Violet's chair
'This is my cello'
She touches soft his hair
'It's over 200 years old
I'm going to play it for you'
She stares at some point distant
And smiles, *'they usually do!'*

Bright strings stirring
Sailor's hornpipe zings
Violet stops stroking
Irene starts to sing
'I am dancing, look I can really dance
I can dance for you, I can twirl and prance
Am I doing good, can I do it right?
Oh I like to dance I can dance all night'
We all move to the horn-pipe sound
A million memories lost and found
Clapping and clicking and shaking withered limbs
Laughing and living out a hundred hungry hymns

A Mum's Moans

Today I listened to a mum
Who nagged and shouted day and night;
As soon as sleep was rubbed from eyes
'Til back in bed and off with light.

"Don't hang about! Get washed and dressed!
You children make me so depressed!
Breakfast time -come down here now!
Don't answer back! There'll be a row!
Look at the time - you're late again!
Not those shoes – look at the rain!
Clean your teeth! Brush that hair!
That coat is just not fit to wear!

So struggling up the hill to school
With bags and boxes clutched in hands,
I listened while their mother moaned
And chided, shouting her demands.

"Get moving – don't just stand and stare!
That bell's gone now and we're not there!
No pocket money from today!
You'll have to learn the time some way!"

At last, at school, a quick farewell –
"You've got to go!" – a hurried kiss.
She set off back across the fields
How dare they make her cross like this!
All back at home, now ten to four,
"Come in- quickly! Shut that door!

Don't run off – here, read to me!
Hurry up! It's time for tea!
Set the table! Pick that up!
Use your fork, you mucky pup!
Now wash your hands! What a mess!
In your hair and down your dress!
No, don't go out! It's time for bed!
Where have you been? I never said!
Come on, now – I've lots to do!
I can't stay here all night with you!"
At last, all safely tucked in bed.
She went downstairs, her work to start.
I saw her stop and wipe her eyes
Then tears flowed from her broken heart.
"My precious ones!" she cried and cried.
"I love them dearly!" How she sighed!
"All I've done today is nag!
What a crotchety old bag!
My treasures, oh so dear to me!
I'll lose them for eternity
If I don't show my love right now
And learn to guide them gently - how?

She lightly stepped up on the stairs
And knelt beside each bed, and hers
And prayed, "Dear God, please help me to
Love these precious gifts from you!"

When that was done, she wrote this line –
Her tale is told, her pen is mine.
Kath Dredge

Diagnosis cancer

Forced along the desolate ridge
Slick with ice and glaring snow,
Eyes closed against the destination.
Afraid.

Down one cliff face,
The slug black abyss of madness beckons.
Shrieked obscenities and agonised howls
Claw up exposed ankles.

False light pales the other slope
Devoid of hope or purpose
A sterile prison
Where robots serve time.

Reach up and cling to
The Father's finger
With tiny human hands.
His Word a ladder,
To scale sky-scraping boulders.
Brothers and sisters
An imperfect bridge from which
To glimpse the crown of life.

K.B. Walker

A Sample Quiet Day

PATHWAYS – A JOURNEY TO THE INNER SELF

"One's own self is well hidden from one's own self;
of all mines of treasure,
one's own is the last to be dug up."
Friedrich Wilhelm Nietzsche

This is a Quiet Day that I put together a number of years ago and one that I have led on a number of occasions. It is based on extracts from C. S. Lewis's book **'The Lion, the Witch and the Wardrobe'**. It can be used on your own, if you would like to spend a day in quiet reflection and prayer, or it can be used for a group of people who wish to come together to explore what might be hidden deep within. Please use it as best suits you and I do pray that it will be a blessing for you.

When we choose to take 'time out' and spend time in quiet reflection it can create within us a deeper awareness of the mystery of ourselves and the mystery of God. Such time gives us the opportunity to let go of all that impedes us from listening to the messages around us. By slowing down and becoming aware of our body, mind and spirit we allow ourselves to think about our calling in life and the role of God and of His Spirit within it.

To help us to begin to prepare for the day it is good to start the quiet time with some kind of relaxation exercise. One suggestion would be to use the act of breathing as a way of focussing the mind to help us relax:

Find a comfortable position for you – it could be seated in a chair or maybe on a cushion on the floor; it might be lying down; it might be kneeling, you decide. When you are ready allow your eyes to gently close. Now, become aware of your breathing. Focus on the air as it enters your body; feel the rise and fall of your chest with each breath and imagine that you are breathing in God's peace and breathing out any concerns or worries you might have. Inevitably you will find your mind will wander, each time it does, gently bring it back to focus on your breathing allowing the wandering thoughts to drift away as if on a cloud. As you persevere you will find that your concentration will be become more clear and stable. If, during this time, you find that you become a little sleepy gently lift your eyes upwards, or, if your mind becomes agitated, turn your eyes slightly downward and let any inner tension dissolve.

This relaxation exercise should take about 10 minutes. When you feel that you have become more relaxed and focussed say a prayer asking for God's blessing on the day, ask for His guidance and for help to open your heart and mind to Him and to what He might wish to impart to you.

'Pathways - The Journey into our Inner Self' – Part 1

 I believe that each of us follows many pathways in our lives, pathways that shape us into the people we are today. Many of these pathways are external – set by the work we do, the church, our family, our friends, our colleagues and the events that happen in our lives. But there is also the journey inwards – the journey into our inner self, our inner world where we can encounter so many emotions, so many thoughts and, ultimately, that great force that motivates our very lives. Most world religions have the concept of a world within where we can encounter our true selves, our inner spirit, our God. This is not a world that is easily accessed and many people might even deny that it even exists. Yet this inner journey begins as soon as we turn our mind on what is within us. It may begin as a conscious act, such as prayer or meditation, through a retreat from everyday life or through the creative exploration of our own imagination. It is a journey that often begins in childhood when we read our first fairy story – especially those that talk of the triumph of good over evil.

Today we are to look at a story that mirror this inner journey and the battles that have to be fought and won if we are to make our way to the centre where love and goodness dwell. The story is one of my favourite children's books it is C S Lewis' 'The Lion, the Witch and the Wardrobe' for here we have a wonderful story of a journey to another land – the land of Narnia.

Four children, Peter, Susan, Edmond and Lucy, have been evacuated from London during the war and they are now living in a large house owned by an old professor. One day the four children decided to explore the house and C. S. Lewis writes:

'.... the children looked into a room that was quite empty except for one big wardrobe; the sort that has a looking glass in the door. 'Nothing there' said Peter and they all trooped out again – all except Lucy (the youngest). She stayed behind because she thought it would be worthwhile trying the door of the wardrobe, even though she felt almost sure that it would be locked. To her surprise it opened quite easily and two mothballs dropped out.
Looking into the inside she saw several coats hanging up – mostly long fur coats. There was nothing Lucy liked so much as the smell and feel of fur. She immediately stepped into the wardrobe and got in among the coats and rubbed her face against them, leaving the door open of course because she knew that it is very foolish to shut oneself into any wardrobe. Soon she went further in and found that there was a second row of coats hanging up behind the first one. It was almost quite dark in there and she

kept her arms stretched out in front of her so as not to bump her face into the back of the wardrobe. She took a step further in – then two or three steps- always expecting to feel woodwork against the tips of her fingers. But she could not feel it.

'This must be a simply enormous wardrobe!' thought Lucy, going still further in and pushing the soft folds of the coats aside to make room for her. Then she noticed that there was something crunching under feet. 'I wonder is that more moth-balls?' she thought, stooping down to feel it with her hands. But instead of feeling the hard, smooth wood of the floor of the wardrobe, she felt something soft and powdery and extremely cold. 'This is very queer', she said, and went on a step or two further.

Next moment she found that what was rubbing against her face and hands was no longer soft fur but something hard and rough and even prickly. 'Why, it is just like branches of trees!' exclaimed Lucy. And then she saw that there was a light ahead of her, not a few inches away where the back of the wardrobe ought to have been, but a long way off. Something cold and soft was falling on her. A moment later she found that she was standing in the middle of a wood at night-time with snow under her feet and snowflakes falling through the air.

Lucy felt a little frightened, but she felt very inquisitive and excited as well. She looked back over her shoulder and there, between the dark tree trunks, she could still see the open doorway of the wardrobe and even catch a glimpse of the empty room from which she had set out – 'I can always get back if anything goes wrong', thought Lucy and she began to walk forward, crunch-crunch over the snow and through the wood towards the other light.'

… thus started the great adventure of discovering Narnia.

Here we have a wonderful story of how the four children each found Narnia in their own way and how each of them reacted to what they had found. Lucy found her way there because she was inquisitive about a new pathway she had found. She stumbled on it by pure chance and she was excited by it all, wanting to see as much as she could and find out as much as she could. There is an innocence about her and she takes everything at face value and follows where she is led. Later, when she gets back to the house none of the other three believe her and she is very hurt and upset by this. Some while later Edmund follows Lucy to the wardrobe and much to his utter astonishment, he too finds his way to

Narnia. However, his experience is very different to Lucy's. He comes across the White Witch who calls herself the Queen of Narnia. She bribes him with hot drinks and Turkish delight. Edmund takes what he can from her; he is selfish and only thinking of himself and what he can get out of it, even to the point that he flatly denies having been through the wardrobe when Lucy tries to convince Peter and Susan of the existence of this new and wonderful world. Peter and Susan are older and they seem to have lost some of their childlike innocence, the presence of another world through the wardrobe is just not logical so they do not believe it. The Professor, however, does believe in this magical land, but he has never found his way there. He knows it in his head, but has not found it in his heart. Of course, Peter and Susan do eventually find their way there when all four children are hiding from the Professor's housekeeper Mrs Macready and all bundle themselves into the wardrobe and thus they find themselves in the fascinating world of Narnia and the four of them have many adventures.

The first period of quiet reflection

This morning, if it is helpful for you, I would like to suggest that you think about that inner journey – your inner journey. Is it a journey that you are already on? If it is, then maybe try to focus on how you found the entrance to this inner world. Did you find it by accident? Did others talk to you about it and give you the courage you needed to start the journey? Are you like the professor – in your mind you know that there is this wonderful inner world, but as yet you have not found the key to getting into it? When you are journeying into this inner world, how do you react? With logical analysis? With excitement and innocence? Do you hide away and keep it to yourself, not wishing to share it with others, for whatever reason?

If you have not yet tried to embark on this journey then think of the reasons why this might be the case. What is stopping you: fear, lack of time; lack of opportunity; unsure where to start; too many thoughts in your head; the fear of making the journey on your own – loneliness?

What might help you to start the journey? What could you try to use?

Some suggestions might be to look at nature and lose yourself in its beauty. Or you could read an uplifting passage from Scripture, one that is meaningful to you, and let it transport your thoughts or your imagination to another world. Maybe you could listen to some beautiful music and lose yourself in its melody. Please don't try too hard to find answers, allow them to pop into your mind and then jot them down or make a mental note of them. This is not supposed to be hard work, just a time of quiet when you allow your heart and mind to speak to you.

'Pathways - The Journey into our Inner Self' – Part 2

One of the subjects that many spiritual teachers talk or write about is discernment, discerning what is from God and what is not; what is good and helpful and what is bad and extremely unhelpful. Our journey to our inner world will bring up so many thoughts and feelings and we need to find ways of discerning which are from God and which are not. Help in this process can come from the most unexpected of sources:

When, eventually, all the children find their way through the wardrobe to Narnia they come across so many creatures, some helpful, some not. Lucy, on her first sortie to this strange land had come across a faun, Mr Tumnus. He had been helpful and she was sure that he would help them all now if only she could find him again:

Lucy sees a robin – 'Look! There's a robin with such a red breast. It's the first bird I've seen here. I say! I wonder can birds talk in Narnia? It almost looks as if it wanted to say something to us.' Then she turned to the robin and said, 'Please, can you tell us where Tumnus the Faun has been taken to?' As she said this she took a step towards the bird. It at once flew away but only as far as the next tree. There it perched and looked at them very hard as if it understood all they had been saying'.

So the children followed the bird until Edmund says to Peter

'We're following a guide we know nothing about. How do we know which side that bird is on? Why shouldn't it be leading us into a trap?'

Peter replies 'That's a nasty idea. Still – a robin, you know. They're good birds in all the stories I've ever read. I'm sure a robin wouldn't be on the wrong side'.

So the children trusted what they already knew and believed to be true, just a tiny little bird. But, it could have been just a tiny little thought or a tiny little idea. Sometimes we have to follow and trust and sometimes we won't know whether the thought or idea is good until it takes us to its destination. In the case of the children the robin led them to the Beavers who proved to be very supportive and helpful. And it was the beavers who really saw the potential within the four children, what they were destined to be.

In the story Edmund decided to follow his own pathway. He ran away from the others because all he could think about was the wonderful Turkish Delight he had enjoyed, which the White Witch had given him. Sadly, his adventure was to prove very difficult and not at all what he had hoped as the witch only wanted to get the four children together and she treated Edmund very badly when she failed to get what she wanted.

The Beavers, however, were very good with the other three children. They helped them all through some very dark and difficult times and helped them on a journey that eventually led them to meet the great Aslan. During their journeys each of them learned much about themselves and their particular gifts.

We are told that they came across Father Christmas:

'Here are your presents,' said Father Christmas – 'and they are tools not toys. The time to use them is perhaps near at hand. Bear them well.' With these words he handed to Peter a shield and a sword. The shield was the colour of silver and across it there ramped a red lion, as bright as a ripe strawberry at the moment when you pick it. The hilt of the sword was of gold and it had a sheath and a sword belt and everything it needed, and it was just the right size and weight for Peter to use. Peter was silent and solemn as he received these gifts, for he felt they were a very serious kind of present. 'Susan, Eve's daughter,' said Father Christmas, 'These are for you,' and he handed her a bow and a quiver full of arrows and a little ivory horn. 'You must use the bow only in great need,' he said, 'for I do not mean you to fight in the battle. It does not easily miss. And when you put this horn to your lips and blow it, then, wherever you are, I think help of some kind will come to you. 'Last of all he said, 'Lucy, Eve's daughter,' and Lucy came forward. He gave her a little bottle of what looked like glass (but people said afterwards that it was made of diamond) and a small dagger. 'In this bottle,' he said, 'there is a cordial made of the juice of one of the fire-flowers that grow in the mountains of the sun. If you or any of your friends is hurt, a few drops of this will restore them. And the dagger is to defend you at great need. For you also are not to be in the battle'.

So the children were given all they needed to face what the future brought to them and each of them made their way to their destination in their own unique way. Peter, Susan and Lucy remained together, Edmund having to fight different battles on his own. Along their way they met creatures that were obviously bad and others they mistook as being bad when they were not – like the fox that protected them from the wolves. In the end they were to see the great goodness of Aslan and how he was prepared to die to save them. They saw goodness overcoming evil and the ability and sacrifice of so many who were prepared to see love prevail. The four children became Kings and Queens and their destiny was fulfilled, they became what they were meant to be:

Peter became a tall and deep-chested man and a great warrior, and he was called King Peter the Magnificent. And Susan grew into a tall and graceful woman with black hair that fell almost to her feet and the kings of the countries beyond the sea began to send ambassadors asking for her hand in marriage. And she was called Susan the Gentle. Edmund was a graver and quieter man than Peter, and great in council and judgement. He was called King Edmund the Just. But, as for Lucy, she was always gay and golden-haired, and all the princes in those parts desired her to be their queen, and her own people called her Queen Lucy the Valiant.

The children's journey into and through Narnia was life changing, just as our journey through life and, in particular, our inner life can be for us.

The second period of quiet reflection

During this time maybe you could begin to reflect on your own journey. These reflections may very well continue for a long time after today for there is so much that each of us will have journeyed through. So many people who have been with us along the way, so many battles we will have fought, won or lost.

To help you in your reflections begin by looking for the little robins: the people, the ideas, the readings, and the thoughts that have skipped ahead of you and gently shown you the way forward. Then look at the things that were so obviously of great help to you, the beavers: the people who have walked some of the journey with you, who helped you, fed you (in whatever way) and enabled you to find your way towards the light – to love, to God.

Think of the gifts that have been given to you that have helped you along the journey.

Think of the pathways that you have taken, or the people who you have met or the ideas you have had that have not been helpful. For even they have formed part of your journey.

And finally, if you were a King or a Queen what would others call you?

To Close

Once you feel that your time of reflection has naturally drawn to end now is the time to offer thanks to God for all the insights you have received. You might decide to use an evening liturgy to help you focus your prayers or you might find that you wish to say a few words of your own born out of all that has happened to you on this day. Finally ask for God's blessing on yourself and your life. Invite Him to accompany you on your continuing journey and ask for His help and strength to guide you.

You might find that a time of meditation will help you to make the transition from the quiet of the day to the busyness of your everyday life. To do this might I suggest that you sit yourself on a chair and, when ready, close your eyes.

For a short while focus on your breathing until you feel more focussed. Now I would like you to imagine that it is very early morning. It is still dark but you can hear the beginnings of the dawn chorus as the birds begin to awaken to their new day. As you listen and look you can see a lightening of the sky towards the East, there is a wonderful golden glow stretching across the horizon as the sun begins to slowly rise. Watch as the sun makes its way up into the sky. You see the sky become lighter and the heat of the sun begins to gently warm your face. You begin to feel brighter, full of energy and ready to awaken to a new phase in your day and in your life. Lift your eyes upwards, assume a straighter posture and open your eyes feeling refreshed and renewed and ready to continue your day.

I do hope that the process of the day has been a blessing to you and that it has helped you along the wonderful journey to your inner self, a journey we often neglect. As St Augustine wrote:

"People go abroad to wonder at the heights of mountains, at the huge waves of the sea, at the long courses of the rivers, at the vast compass of the ocean, at the circular motions of the stars, and they pass by themselves without ever wondering.'

Susan Brooks
Spiritual Director & Retreat Giver